Tiny
Conversations

by

Kerrie Carnes Salwa

Tiny Conversations, Published February, 2015

Interior and Cover Illustrations: Geralyn Miller
Interior Layout: Howard Johnson, Howard Communigrafix, Inc.
Author Photo: Coellyn McIninch
Editorial: Susan Herbert
Proofreading: Karen Grennan
Conversation Titles: Tom Flanagan

 SDP Publishing

Published by SDP Publishing, an imprint of SDP Publishing Solutions, LLC.

To obtain permission(s) to use material from this work, please submit a written request to:

SDP Publishing
Permissions Department
PO Box 26, East Bridgewater, MA 02333
or email your request to info@SDPPublishing.com.

Library of Congress Control Number: 2014959264

ISBN-13 (print): 978-0-9913167-6-2
ISBN-13 (ebook): 978-0-9913167-7-9
Printed in the United States of America

Acknowledgments

You can't survive five years with a life this crazy without having a few thank yous to pass out. This may be my only book, so I have to make them count. Here is my list:

Thank you to my mother … for her backbone and all of her prayers for my survival.

Thank you to my sisters, both here and gone, for never leaving my side.

Thank you to my family for helping on a moment's notice.

Thank you to my in-laws for being so normal.

Thank you to my girlfriends for always letting me vent.

Thank you to my Breast Intentions team for keeping me focused.

Thank you to Karen McManimon for always being my cheerleader.

Thank you to MaryKate Winn for always allowing me to choose the twins.

Thank you to Seth "Seth Peter" Salwa for our broke but happy life.

And a very special thank you to Tom Flanagan for his time, wit, and sense of humor on this project and for titling our tiny conversations.

*I dedicate this book to my
Tree Frog and my Moon Ninja—the two coolest girls
I know.*

The Story

So, first comes stalking, I mean love, then comes marriage, then comes … oh, I guess it is not that easy to have a baby! Like a lot of other people realize, after years of trying every way possible to *prevent* pregnancy, actually getting pregnant isn't really as easy as you thought. So we did what any normal people already in decent careers would do—we bought our favorite bar. Our favorite dive bar at that!

After months of preparing, researching, and business plan writing, The Spillway was ours! The doors opened and everything was great. Then a couple of months later, I was in a kickboxing class and nearly passed out. That's right … pregnant!

About two months after that I got the news … twins! Seth's first response to the news, in front of a full Emergency Room, was, "We have to buy a house. I'm going to need a bigger truck. We have to sell the bar!!!"

Soon after *that* surprise, we did end up buying a house. We got settled in and had our twin girls, Natalie and Abby. We did not, however, end up selling the bar.

Within one year we had two kids, a house, and a bar. Being at home with the girls, juggling the bar business, and taking care of the house was very overwhelming to me. In some cases I could even consider it a blur.

On top of the normal day-to-day struggles of owning and operating a business, caring for two babies, and keeping up a household, we had other not-too-typical hardships on our plate. My mother, who had been previously diagnosed with and had beaten lung cancer in 1999, was diagnosed for a second time with a very rapid growing skin cancer in her right armpit. She underwent surgery and several more rounds of radiation. She is now considered in recovery, yet left with a lifetime of lympodema as a reminder of her conquest. My father was given his very own lung cancer diagnosis while Seth and I were on our honeymoon in 2005. A man of more than nine lives fought the good fight until he passed away in 2011. My oldest sister, Kathy, didn't make it to see The Spillway or meet the twins, even though the girls swear they met her before they were born. She also died of cancer in 2004 at the age of 39.

When the girls started talking, I started posting some of the funny things they would say on my Facebook page for two reasons: 1) When you own a bar (this was not in the classes or research) you don't realize how many times you have to have the SAME CONVERSATIONS with people over and over and over. It is borderline exhausting. The Facebook posts allowed people to get to know the girls in such a way that they didn't have to ask me the same questions all the time. 2) I realized quickly that sharing these with the public took my mind off the harsh reality that my life had become stressful to an extreme and scary level.

The "tiny conversations" posts began with this one when the girls were two, and we were sitting down in the kitchen during snack time. Natalie hummed her yogurt across the room into the pantry door. I know I said a lot of this was a blur, but I do remember this like it was yesterday.

Me: Natalie, do you know why you are in a time out?

Natalie: Yes. I know why I am in a time out.

Me: Well, why?

Natalie: Because I threw my yogurt across the kitchen.

Me: Natalie, what in the world would make you do something like that?

Natalie: Because it wasn't PINK!

And so it began ...

Redecorating a TV and a Twin

Me: Nat, why do you have glitter on your lips?

Natalie: It's my nail polish.

Me: Where did you get it?

Natalie: My pocketbook.

Me: OMG, what else did you put it on besides your lips?

Natalie: Abby.

Me: Anything else?

Natalie: The TV.

Me: The one we just bought two days ago?

Natalie: Yes, that one.

Mysterious Chinese Friends

Me: Girls, we're going to Worcester to Maddie's softball game.

Abby: I wanna go to China.

Me: We're going to Worcester.

Abby: But I wanna go to China.

Me: It's too far of a flight, and I have no interest in going there. I'm sorry, but Worcester it is.

Natalie: Don't worry, Abby, Mr. Han (from the *Karate Kid* remake) can help us get to China.

No Party, Big Problem

Me: You girls know today is Uncle Bee's birthday?

Natalie: Uncle Bee??

Abby: Yeah, you know … Winnie's husband?

Abby: Is it time to go to his party??

Me: There is no party.

Abby: Oh, man.

Good Night's Sleep

Natalie: Did I sleep in my own bed?

Me: Yes.

Settling for New Hampshire

Natalie: Do we have school today?

Me: No.

Natalie: Are we going on a Disney cruise?

Me: No!!

Natalie: New Hampshire with our cousins?

Me: Yes.

Find a Penny

Natalie: DADDY!

Seth: Yes, Natalie?

Natalie: Can you come here?

Seth: Yes. Where are you?

Natalie: I'm upstairs going potty!

Seth: You need help?

Natalie: NO! I found a penny, and I need you to bring me up a scratch ticket!

A Brother or a *Brother?*

Natalie: When you get us a brother, can you get us one that's brown?

Me: Like, brown hair?

Natalie: No. Like brown all over.

Puppy Love

Natalie: Mommy, instead of a puppy, can we get a porcupine?

No Love

Me: I love you, Abby.

Abby: I love Josie. (her daycare provider)

Sleep On It

Things Natalie asked me while I was trying to put her to sleep one night:

    1) Do you think I look like you?

    2) Why would anybody play the accordion?

    3) When we wake up, can I show you my new funny faces?

    4) Can you please put us in a dance class?

Pierced Bellies

Natalie: If I sleep good tonight, Mom, can I get my ears pierced?

Me: Yes, Lovey, we've already discussed this.

Natalie: Well, if I sleep in my bed all month, can I get my belly button pierced?

Me: (ballistic) NO, NO, NO! No way!

Natalie: You forgot Jose.

Helping Each Other Learn to Swear

Natalie: Dangnabit.

Abby: No, Natalie, it's damn rabbit.

Mall Before Sunrise?

6:19 a.m.

Natalie: Mommy, did I sleep all night in my bed all by myself?

Seth and Me: (massive celebration) Yes, Love.

Natalie: Can we go to the mall and get my ears pierced now?

3:45 a.m.

Me: Nat, Mommy has to go to work in the morning and you have to go to school, so it's important that we get our rest. Plus, you promised you'd sleep in your own bed all night.

Natalie: Well, you promised I could get my ears pierced and they aren't pierced.

Mother of the Year

Me: Abby, what is that I keep hearing you say?

Abby: Frick it!

Me: Oh ... yikes.

Spreading Germs and Love

Me: I think I caught you guys' colds.

Natalie: Did you get it from loving us?

Well, You Asked

Me: So ... what is your full name? Is it Abigail or Abby?

Abby: Actually, it's Abby Kathleen Salwa.

Buddy the Elf (Take 1)

Abby: Can you tell us the story?

Me: It's really late, you guys. We have to go straight to bed tonight.

Natalie: Well, if you aren't going to tell us the story of Cinderella, can you please explain to us how Elf is an elf?

Abby: Yeah, where does him live and how come him doesn't have a mom?

Random Statements

Natalie: Mom, you make me so happy.

Abby: Mom, I'm just gonna go in and chill for a minute, ok?

Can't Rub Two Pennies Together

So, I bring Abby with me into Meadowbrook one night to get a juice and some gum (total $3.45). I open my wallet to pay the girl, and I have two fives (to my name, mind you). I give one five to the girl ringing us up, and Abby very politely grabs the other five and puts it in her TIP JAR!!!!

Valley Girl at Age 3

Natalie: Mooooom, I have a bosquito bite and it hurts more than anything else in my entirrrre life.

Fists Flying, Kids Crying

Me: Abby, what just happened?

Abby: Natalie gave me a knuckle sandwich, and now I'm cryyyyinggg.

Hooked on Phonics?

Natalie: (just woke up from a nap in car) Mom, is this Cape Cod?

Me: Yes, Baby. How did you know that?

Natalie: It says it in those bushes over there.

Me: W.T.F.

Huge Pink Heart

Natalie: I'm going to paint the whole world pink!

Fairy Tale Life on Schley Street

Abby: Mom, you're really lucky.

Me: How's that Ab?

Abby: You are living happily ever after.

Me: Speechless.

Cry, Baby, Cry

While Natalie was pitching a fit from being overtired:

Me: Are you gonna do this all day?

Natalie: (through the tears) No, I'm almost done.

Buddy the Elf (Take 2)

At the bar with the girls:

Me: Natalie, do not touch that gum from under the table!! That's so gross.

Natalie: Well, Elf does.

Baby Brother Request #45

Natalie: Kerrie Carnes Salwa, can you get us a little brudder?

Me: No way, Jose.

Natalie: Well, Cullan has one and Makena and Kaleigh and Paige all have one.

Me: (thinking) And so it begins …

Old Soul

Abby: I'm just gonna take a few deep breaths and start again.

Me: Great idea, Ab.

Conversations with Stinky Lizzy

Me: How did it go today with the girls?

Lizzy: It was going great, and then Natalie asked me, "Where did you get your arse?"

OCD Much?

Natalie: Mom, do you think we could try to not be late for swim lessons today. Maybe we could get there when it starts?

Brutally Honest

Natalie: You're really, really big and you're really, really fat.

Me: Today is gonna be a great day. I can feel it.

3 Going on 30

Me: (in a tizzy) Natalie! Do you think I do this for my health?

Natalie: Actually, I'm not sure what that means, Mom.

Daddy Knows Best

Seth: Natalie, you are a very, very good girl, you know that?

Natalie: Yeah, I guess I am.

Sleepless on Schley

Natalie: I just can't … I just can't do it.

Me: Do what?

Natalie: Sleep!!!!

Party Rockers in the House ... Again?

Driving down Church Street one night:

Abby: Mom, can you believe those people are having a party AGAIN???

Me: That's not a house, Love. It's a funeral home.

3:15 a.m.

Natalie: (in a very loud whisper) Mom, I'm awake.

Me: I see that.

Natalie: Well, I'm done sleeping.

Me: Is that so?

Natalie: I was thinking we could go downstairs and watch the Justin Bieber movie?

Me: (shaking my head)

Ohh La La

Natalie: You have really nice boobs, Mom.

Me: You're my favorite child, Natalie.

Barbie Movies Are a No-No

Natalie: You're ruining my life, Mom!

Me: Good. Pretty sure that is my job as a mother.

Drew—the Little Cutie

Me: Girls, let's go to the playground and play with our friends.

Abby: Is Drew gonna be there? You know ... Drew, the little cutie.

Me: Think so.

Abby: (smile)

Sleepover Shenanigans

After a sleepover at my brother, Johnny's, house:

Johnny: I thought you said the girls have to wait until they're five to chew gum.

Me: I did.

Johnny: Oh. Natalie said she can chew GUM, she just has to wait until she is five to chew BUBBLE gum.

Hair Did

Me: Abby, c'mon. It's your turn to get your hair done.

Abby: Ok. But I'm gonna need A LOT of product today, Mommy.

Brother ... Again?

Abby: Mommy, I want a baby brother this size (points to her baby doll). Can you buy me one?

Me: Honey, I told you that you can't buy baby brothers ...

Abby: Oh yeah, I remember ... If everyone sleeps in their own bed, then your belly gets really big, and then POOF! You have a baby brother.

The Biebs

Abby: Mom. Do you know who Selena Gomez is?

Me: Yes.

Abby: Can you even BELIEVE she is Justin Bieber's girlfriend?

3:15 a.m.

Natalie: Mum, when is Arbor Day?!

Me: What? Go to bed Natalie.

Natalie: You know, Arbor Day.

Me: Ugh. I know. I don't know when it is. Good night!

Natalie: Well, can we dig for worms at Nana's tomorrow?

Me: Yes, but only if you go to sleep.

Natalie: I hope she has wood chips to look under.

Busted!

Abby: Mommy! Your feet are sooo dirty!

Me: Ugh, I know. It's from dance, dance, dancing last night.

Abby: Were you a dancing machine?

Me: I was.

Abby: Wait, Mommy, you said you were going to work last night!

Ask Grammy

Natalie: Grammy, have you ever been to Neverland?

Gram: No. No, I haven't.

Natalie: Then … can you tell me about Betty Boop?!?

Why Are There So Many Songs About Rainbows?

4:15 a.m.

Natalie: MOMMY!

Me: (awoken out of a dead sleep) What, Natalie?

Natalie: Can you sing me the song from the Muppet movie?

Me: Ugh, Natalie, it's 4:15 in the morning!

Natalie: No, it's four-one-three. (different clock)

Me: Go to bed, Natalie. Plllleeeassseee??

Me: Ma na ma naw.

Natalie: No, the rainbow one.

Nerds

Me: Girls! What do you think you are going to learn about today at school? (silence)

Natalie: Ahh … Maybe about how the sun is a giant ball of fire and the biggest star and how the planets orbit.

Me: Oh, is that all?

Abby: And then we'll probably play outside or make more astronauts.

One of My All-time Faves

I was cooking dinner and the twins were on the stairs. I went to let them know dinner was ready.

Me: Natalie, what are you holding? (I could tell from the bottom of the stairs it was our mortgage payment.)

Natalie: I opened an email for you. Looks like we won a trip to Disney!!!

2:30 a.m.

Natalie: (whispers) MOM, DO YOU THINK I CAN TAKE YOUR PHONE TO SCHOOL ONE DAY AND SHOW MY FRIENDS WHO BETTY BOOP IS BECAUSE THEY DON'T KNOW WHO SHE IS.

Me: I bet Josie would looovvve that Natalie. GO TO BED!

Road TRIP!

Me: C'mon girls, get in the car. Mommy has a surprise for you!

Natalie: Are we going to Lowe's?

Abby: Or Texas Road House?

Natalie: Disney on Ice, maybe?

Abby: Are we going to Cleveland???

Me: (uh-oh) Actually, we are going to pick out dresses for you. (at a consignment shop)

Teacher, Teacher!

Natalie: Abby, you sleep like a champ. Can you teach me how to sleep?

Abby: Sure, Natalie. All you have to do is close your eyes and keep 'em closed.

Natalie: Can you teach me how to sleep the whole time?

Abby: Sure. When your eyes open, you just shut them right away so that your eyes are shut in a straight line. Just like that!

Our First Boston Marathon

Me: Girls, the marathon is about to start and the really fast runners I was telling you about are gonna be coming by!!

Abby: You mean Kelly Duffy?

Me: I was talking about the Africans. But maybe Kelly Duffy. You never know.

First Overnight to Grammy's!

Me: So … can they sleep over ever again?

Gram: Yes, of course. In like 6 months?

Hip Hop Twins

So I was putting the girls to bed one night (in their non-bunked bunk beds). They were almost asleep in the pitch dark when from one bed I heard "boom shakalaka" and from the opposite bed I heard "shakalaka boom." I couldn't make this stuff up.

Sticks and Stones

Me: Abby!! Come inside. There are a million bees out there. Shut the door!

Natalie: You're so mean to her, Mommy.

Me: No, I'm not.

Natalie: Yes, you are.

Me: No, I'm not.

Natalie: You're super mean.

Me: YOU'RE wicked mean.

Natalie: You're MEGA mean!!

People of Target

Abby: Sorry I acted like a crazy person at Target today, Mom.

The Heat Is On

Abby: Mommy, who invented heat?

Me: Ummm ... Barry Whitney. (the owner of our local heating company)

Revelation

After a week of trying to "super nanny" the girls to bed with only one night of success, I admitted defeat and laid down with them.

Natalie: Mummy, I know that it upsets you that we can't go to sleep on our own, but we can't sleep without you and we hate, HATE going to bed alone. We really love you, and we are happy you are going to sleep with us tonight.

1) Now I feel like an a-hole.

2) Now I have to try to run my business and make decisions via text from the CRACK of two twin beds pushed together.

3) Notice all the "we" talk. I guarantee you Abby could fall asleep ON THE MOON by herself and wouldn't care.

4) I wouldn't trade my life for all the tea in China.

Secret Passwords

Natalie: Can I use the camera?

Abby: No, you need a password.

Natalie: Well, what is it?

Abby: The password?

Natalie: Yes!

Abby: Ok, it's "Daddy's got a stinky bum."

2nd Favorite

Abby: Mommy, I love you.

Me: I love you too, Baby.

Abby: I love you to the moon!

Me: I love YOU to the moon!

Abby: I love you like a love song, Baby.

We Love Vermont

Abby: Mom, do we have school tomorrow?

Me: Yes, two more days.

Abby: Then woo-hoo Vermont???!?

Me: Yes, then woo-hoo Vermont.

Natalie: I can't wait to ride my bike down the mountain.

Me: Um … Have you been talking to Daddy?

Natalie: Then can we go on the mountain coaster?

Abby: Or are we just gonna chill, baby, chill?

6:45 a.m.

Natalie: Mommy!! Did we sleep in our own beds all night long?

Me: Yes, Lovey, you did!! We are so proud of you guys.

Abby: I was so very scared in my bed last night!

Me: You were? What happened?

Abby: It was dark, and I was scared, so Natalie came into my bed with me.

Clinton= 5.2 Square Miles, Mind You

Natalie: I just love you so much, Mom. I do. I love you to the other side of this whole world!

Me: I love you too, Natalie. That was very sweet. Thank you for such a great Mother's Day.

Abby: Well, I love you to the other side of Clinton, MASS!

Me: Whoa, thanks, Abby. You guys are the greatest.

Dora the Explorer?

Natalie: (whispering, at bedtime) We are your little mojitos.

Me: What did you say, Love?

Natalie: We are your little mojitos.

Me: (thinking) I know these two grew up in a bar, but we don't even serve mojitos there!

1:05 a.m.

Natalie: Mom! I'm here.

Me: Great.

Natalie: And look ... I brought Abby!

Me: Awesome.

Buddy the Elf (Take 3)

Me: Natalie, sorry I was so impatient just now. I should have waited until after you guys went to bed to do the computer stuff.

Abby: Did you not mean to say all the stuff to me, Mom?

Me: Yes, Abby. I'm sorry I was so impatient.

Natalie: It's ok, Mom. I love you. (then whispers) All the way to California! San Francisco, California!!

Abby: San Francisco ... That's fun to say!

Spell Check

Abby: Mom. What does D-I-C-K spell?

Me: Ummmm ... Richard!

Boots with Da Fur?

Abby: Hey, Mom.

Me: Hey, Ab.

Abby: I love you, Mom.

Me: I love you too, Abby.

Abby: I love you a ton!

Me: I love YOU a ton!

Abby: Do you love me more than Apple Bottom jeans?

Me: Yes, Love. I definitely do.

Hurricane Sandy Relief Trip

Abby: Mom. What were you doing out there?

Me: I was talking to Uncle Bee.

Abby: What were you talking about?

Me: I was telling him all about my trip.

Natalie: Well, don't you think it would be nice to maybe tell your DAUGHTERS about your trip?!

Show the Love

Abby: Mom, you should really start calling Daddy "Honey" more instead of "Seth Peter."

Don't Eat That

Abby: Mom! I think we need to go grocery shopping.

Me: I know. I'm going this morning.

Natalie: I'd say it's time to go—all we have is applesauce and beer.

First Conversation of the Day

Natalie: You aren't going to heaven today, Mom, are you?

Me: Please don't jinx me, Nat. No, I'm not.

Natalie: I would wicked miss you.

Me: I'm not going anywhere, Love.

Natalie: Do you have to go to the bar?

Me: Well, yeah, I do have to go there. Someone has to clean.

Natalie: You have to clean up after all those stinky boys?

Me: Ha, ha, yeah.

Is That a Fact?

Natalie: I think it's great that you gave us choices. That was nice of you. BUT, I have been dreaming of the Build-A-Bear Workshop for days now, and that is where I want to go.

Me: That wasn't an option.

Natalie: Well, you should make it one.

Hook a Sister Up

Abby: Mom ... can you carry me, PLEASE??!?

Me: Abby, it's 7 a.m. You're tired already??

Abby: Yes. My feet are out of breath!

Trying to Get Natalie to Sleep Last Night

Natalie: Mom. I do not want to go to sleep.

Me: No kidding?

Natalie: I'm not going to sleep at all. I'm going to sit on my bed all night long.

Me: Natalie, it's bedtime (from super nanny). If you don't lie down and go to sleep, I'm leaving.

Natalie: Not gonna do it.

Me: Ok, ONE!

Natalie: Oh, Mom … Don't start with that.

Whatchutalkin' 'Bout?

Abby: Mom. This is the scary part when he gets stoled by the witch.

Me: It's stolen, Honey.

Abby: What?

Me: Instead of saying stoled, you say stolen.

Abby: Is that Chinese?

It's the Sound … of Science

Natalie: How do you get babies in your tummy, Mommy?

Me: Moms just rule, and they have a special space in their belly where babies grow and sleep, and they eat and drink what moms eat and drink.

Natalie: Even BEER???

Are You There DSS? It's Me, Natalie.

Natalie: Mom. Do you think Dora is closer to four years old or more like six years old?

Me: I'd say closer to six.

Natalie: Do you think it's strange that she just wanders off all the time without her parents??

Fatty Boom-balatti

Natalie: Mom, can you come downstairs and cuddle?

Me: I would, Love, but I have to get ready for work.

Natalie: Can I watch you get ready for work?

Me: Sure, just don't play in my make-up.

Natalie: Ok. Wow, Mom. Your belly sure is getting big. Are you sure there isn't a baby brother in there?

Me: No, Natalie, there is no baby in there.

Natalie: But it keeps getting bigger and bigger?

Me: Wait until you see how big it gets when Mommy finally loses her s*#t and instead of eating and drinking like a normal person she has a strict alcohol intake.

Natalie: Then will we have a brother?

Me: Here, play with my make-up.

Friends Who Mass-Produce Kids

Natalie: Can you please get us a baby brother?

Me: Not a chance.

Natalie: It's not fair.

Me: It's perfectly fair.

Natalie: Well, Ann-Marie is having ANOTHER baby. They get a brother.

Me: Well, Ann-Marie Kerrigan Wilson is sick and twisted and Mommy and Daddy aren't.

Nice!

Natalie: Mom. Daddy usually holds our hands when it's dark and we are falling asleep.

Me: Well, Daddy's arms are longer than Mommy's.

Abby: Well. Your BOOBS are bigger than Daddy's!!

Best Quote of Vacation

Abby: MOM, you said your job as our mom was to protect us.

Me: It is!

Abby: Well, how come then I have poison ivy and a thousand bug bites!!?

Literally

Me: You guys, is this an awesome day or what?

Abby: What.

More Geography Majors in the Family

6:00 a.m.

Natalie: I just love you, Mom.

Me: I love you too, Natalie.

Natalie: No, I really love you.

Me: Well, I wicked love you.

Natalie: I love you to Boston.

Me: I love you to California.

Natalie: I love you to Alastica. Is that really far away?

Me: Doesn't get any farther than that.

Natalie: Good.

Mom Can Do Anything!

Me: Natalie. Pick out an outfit to wear so we can go.

Natalie: Ok. I want to wear all green today.

Me: I have a green shirt but no green shorts, pants, or skirts.

Natalie: Well, did you bring your sewing kit?

Me: We are on vacation, Honey. What do you want me to do, make you green shorts?

Natalie: Yes, please.

Dealing with Papa Going to Heaven

Natalie: So, your daddy is in heaven, huh?

Me: Yeah.

Nat: Do you think you'll get a new one?

Me: Nahhh. He was my dad for a really long time and now instead of him, I have really great memories.

(pause)

Natalie: Well, my daddy is in Vermont.

Hey Now

Abby: Mom. After you put us to bed can we sneak into your room to watch the really tall guy with the curly hair?

Me: What? Who are you talking about?

Abby: You know. Daddy's favorite guy ...

Me: HOWARD STERN?

Abby: Yes!!

Me: No!!! You are much too young for Howard Stern. Hey now!

Priorities

Abby: Can we sleep at Nana's tonight while you and Daddy are at the wedding?

Me: YES!! But you have to ask Nana first.

Abby: Ok.

Abby: Actually ... Auntie Becki has a bigger TV. Maybe we could sleep there instead?

Wanna-be Globetrotters

Seth: Girls, if it's nice out after school today we can do something fun!

Natalie: Well, can we go to all the countries in the world?

Short and Sweet

Natalie comes into our room crying and sick:

Me: Is there anything I can do to make you feel better? I hate that you are sick!

Natalie: (still crying) You shouldn't say "hate," Mom. You could sing me a song?

Me: Ok. "Let's start at the very beginning ... it's a very good place to start."

Natalie: (interrupts) Can you sing a song that is a little bit shorter?

Me: Okaaaay. Twinkle twinkle ...

Of All Things

Me: Girls!!! This is it—your big birthday weekend. Can you believe it?

Abby: I feel like we have been waiting FOREVER for this birthday!

Me: I know. What do you guys want to do? We already have a wedding, a funeral, and a birthday party for that day. But what would you like to do?

Natalie: I'm thinking that we could do something really, really, really cool.

Abby: Yeah, me too.

Me: I'm all ears. How do you guys want to celebrate your big 4th birthday?

Natalie: I say definitely doing LAUNDRY!!!

Abby: ME TOO!!!

(What is wrong with these two?)

Big Mac, Filet o' Fish

Abby: Mom. Can we get out of here for a while?

Me: Like the house or Clinton, MASS?

Abby: Both.

Me: Honey, I have to go to work tonight. Where would you like to go? Vermont? Maine?

Abby: I was thinking McDonald's drive thru.

41

This One Is For the Girls with the Boomin' System

Natalie: Mom. We do NOT look awesome today.

Me: Ugh, yeah, you do.

Natalie: No, we don't, and I don't like the things you pick out for me.

Me: Yeah, trust me, I know. You have been telling me that since you learned how to talk.

Natalie: (with attitude) Well?

Me: (with attitude back) Well?

Natalie: Well … can we just listen to Super Bass now?

Foul Mouth

Natalie: Holy shit.

Seth: What did you just say?

Natalie: (mumble)

Seth: What did you just say, Natalie?

Natalie: (mumble again)

Abby: Dad, I think she said OH SHIT!

The New Age

Abby: Where are we going?

Me: To the grocery store.

Abby: Well, I want to go to the app store.

Nothin' but Love

Natalie: Is it morning?

Me: I think so.

Natalie: What do we have to do today? (like ugh …)

Me: NOTHING!! Grammy is here so we can hang out with her this morning.

Natalie: I just love your beautiful mother.

Me: Me too, Lovey. Me too.

YouTube Obsession

Going to bed one night:

Me: Natalie, remember today when we were walking to Daddy's softball game, and we were talking about you and Abby's birthday party coming up?

Natalie: Yes.

Me: When I told you that I didn't know how to make a Barbie cake and you told me to go to bettycrocker.com. How did you know that?

Natalie: It's from the videos I watch on you and Daddy's phones. But, it's actually bettycrockerskitchen.com

Me: Oh, ok, thanks.

Whoops!

Natalie: Mommy, can you play that song again?

Me: Which song, Love?

Natalie: The one that goes "drinkinnnn' all your wine … to take away that paaiaiaiain."

Me: Ummmm. No, Honey, time for school. Chop chop.

1-2-3 Repeater

Abby: Dad … Daddy … Daddy … um … Dad.

 Seth: I'm changing my name.

(pause)

Abby: SETH PETER!!!

So Happy Together

Putting the girls to bed one night:

Abby: Mom, I love you.

Me: I love you, too, Baby.

Abby: I think we need some space.

Me: Um, are we breaking up?

Abby: Not like space like Mars, but space. Like if two people need space … space.

Me: (trying to comprehend) You mean like you and me together space? Like we need to spend time alone together?

Fifth Time Is Charming

Me: Ladies, today is a big day for Mommy at work. I really, really, really, need you to help me out. You need to focus and help me get you ready and out the door in a timely manner and preferably without tears or meltdowns. We cool?

Abby: Yes, Mom.

Natalie: Yes, Mommy.

(30 minutes later—time to go.)

Me: Natalie, I need you to put your other sock on. This is the fifth time I have asked you.

Natalie: (about to lose it while putting on her sock) Ok, Mom, I promise I am not going to spiral on you today.

Ass … No Bueno

Abby: Natalie! Move! You are hurting my ass!!

Seth: Excuse me?!?

Abby: She is hurting my ass!!

Me: Where did you hear that!?!

Abby: What? Ass? It's Spanish for "bum."

Me: Oh, really? Who told you that???

A Sliver of Innocence

Me: Girls, last night was your first night in your new room and you went to bed like big girls all alone! What did you guys talk about?

Abby: Daddy's friend, Jay Flanagan.

Natalie: And how he gave Daddy a sliver in his bum.

Me: Oh, good story. What else did you discuss?

Natalie: We practiced laughing and crying at the same time.

Me: Really? Why is that?

Abby: You said Kathy could do it as a special talent, and we wanted to have it too.

Me: She sure did …

Ab Fab, Sister

Abby: You look fabulous, Natalie. You are going to cry you look so fabulous.

Naggin' the Night Away

5:00 a.m.

Natalie: Mom, Ashlyn and Aubrey are going to be here in five days. We have to really clean this house.

Me: Thanks, Natalie. You sound like my mother. Now go back to sleep.

Natalie: Did your wedding dress have sleeves? Weren't you cold?

Me: It was strapless and 200 degrees.

Potty Words

Abby: Ugh! This stupid phone!

Seth: Abby, don't say stupid.

Abby: Ugh! This damn phone!

Seth: Abby, don't say that either.

Abby: This shitty phone!!

Direct Line to Hollywood

Natalie: Mom, do you think you could do me a favor?

Me: Sure, anything. What do you need?

Natalie: Can you call Justin Bieber?

Me: Ummm … like … on the phone?

Natalie: Yeah, can you ask him if he could come to play at our bar?

Down with Old School Hip-Hop

Abby: Hey, Mom.

Me: Hey, Abby.

Abby: I like the way you work it!! No diggity.

Me: Wow. Thanks, girlfriend!

Jesus and Mary Bedroom

Me: Girls, you are going to be three soon! I think that we should get some new bed sets. What would you like on yours?

Natalie: I want Jesus on mine.

Abby: If she is having Jesus, then I want Mary on mine!

Me: It looks like you two have been spending some time at Grammy's house.

New Job, New Addition

Natalie: (to her girlfriend) Guess what, Katie?

Katie: What?

Natalie: My mom finally got a job, so now we can have a baby.

Katie: You guys are having a baby?

Abby: Well, we say we are, but Mommy keeps telling us to cram it.

Wheeeere's Johnny?

Natalie: Mom, it is not fair that everyone gets to pick us up from school but Uncle Johnny. It is not fair that we have to go all day on Wednesday.

Me: Well, Love, Uncle Johnny works during the day and there isn't anybody to pick you up on Wednesdays.

Natalie: Well, I'm gonna call him and ask him to pick us up next week.

Me: Ok, but don't be disappointed if he can't.

Natalie: Ok.

One Sentence Says It All

Abby: You are the best mother I have ever had.

Uncle Johnny, Part 2—The Conclusion

Johnny: Yeah, so ah … I got a voicemail from Natalie last week.

Me: Yeah, she told me she was going to call you.

Johnny: So I saved it for you. This is what she said: Uncle Johnny, it's me, Natalie. I think you should pick us up at school next week on Wednesday. We are trying to save our parents some money on daycare.

No Cell Towers in Heaven?

Natalie: Mom, is Kathy alive up in Heaven?

Me: Yes. Yes, she is.

Natalie: Oh, cool. So, she is just dead on earth?

Me: Yes, I think you could say that.

Natalie: So, we could call her if we wanted to then?

Me: No, Love, unfortunately, we can't call Heaven.

Natalie: So, you can call China and Oregon and the North Pole, but you can't call Heaven?

Me: Sorry Charlie, but you can't.

Natalie: Well, that is too bad.

Paying the Price for the Little Things

Me: Girls, if you guys can get back into sleeping through the night again maybe we can talk about a sleepover with Katie and Marin at the end of the month.

Natalie: Oh! That would be nice and also … I told Marin if she starts going poop on the potty that I would take her for ice cream.

Natalie, MD

Natalie: Mom, do you still have that rock in your belly?

Me: You mean the kidney stones? Yeah, unfortunately I do.

Natalie: I'm sorry, Mom.

Me: Thanks, Love. I'm going to be fine. I promise.

Natalie: Do you think you got it from screaming at us all the time?

No Cup For You

Abby: MAAA-OOOM!

Me: AABBBBBYYYYY?

Abby: I spilled my drink again.

Me: That's different …

Abby: I know. I'm going to be using a sippy cup until I'm, like, 24.

Savings Bond on a Babysitter

Abby: I can't wait until you are a grandmother and you can babysit so I can go out with my girlfriends.

Shots and Swearing

Me: Girls, if you get all your shots today for kindergarten, then we can do whatever you want today. (It's not a typical approach I use, but the shots were a surprise to them.)

After …

Me: OK, ladies. That was traumatic, but it's over. Now what would you like to do?

Natalie: Anything, really?

Me: Yes, anything.

Abby: I want to eat cake.

Natalie: I want to eat cake and say swears.

Don't Even Ask

Me: Natalie, are those your shoes?

Natalie: No.

Me: Where did you get them?

Natalie: School.

Me: Why didn't you wear your shoes home?

Natalie: Mom, it's a long story.

Birds, Bees, and Ears

Natalie: You always say that you and Dad made us, right?

Me: Sure did.

Natalie: Well, why did you make me with so many ear infections?

Me: That was not our intention, trust me.

Natalie: Where exactly did you make us?

Textbook Backhanded Compliment

Natalie: Mom, you're getting skinny!

Me: Thanks, Love.

Natalie: Well, you still have a long way to go …

Evict 'em All

Me: Abby Kathleen Salwa!!!! If you go out this door without shutting the screen one more time you are going to have to find a new place to live!! That's it!!

Abby: Ohhhh … can I take Natalie with me?

Me: YES! Absolutely.

Jill of Some Trades

Me: Oh, Abby! Your dress is coming undone.

Abby: Well, you'll just have to sew it, Mommy. You're a great sewer.

Me: That's nice, Abby, but Mommy isn't really that good at sewing.

Abby: Well, you are a better sewer than you are a cooker.

Is That One of Those Made-up Twin Words?

Natalie: Good morning, Momma.

Me: Good morning, Love.

Natalie: Don't forget what today is.

Me: I won't. I couldn't.

Natalie: I'm so nervicited!!

What's in a Name

Natalie: What are you looking at?

Me: This is a picture of the little girl I was named after. She was on a show we all used to watch when I was little called *Little House on the Prairie.*

Natalie: Who was I named after?

Me: Natalie Maines. She is a rock star and she is very, very cool.

Natalie: Can I see a picture?

Me: Sure, here she is.

Natalie: I don't even look like her!?!?

Abby: Who was I named after?

Me: A GREAT album called Abbey Road. Here is a picture of it.

Abby: Oh that's nice. Natalie gets named after a pretty girl rock star and I get named after four BOYS!!??!!??

Laughing at Death

Natalie: Mom, are you awake?

Me: Yes, Love. What's up?

Natalie: I'm sorry about Boogers. If I could hug your heart I would.

Me: Ahh … Thank you, Baby. It's okay though. He was a good man, and he had a happy life. We are just going to really miss him, that's all.

Natalie: I couldn't imagine having my own restaurant that I could have mac and cheese any time I wanted. I bet he is gonna miss that.

Surprise—a Sweet Surprise

Abby: Guess what Natalie told me today when we got off the bus after school?

Me: Um, I can only imagine. What did she tell you?

Abby: She told me that she will always be there for me.

Attention to Detail … For Better or Worse

Me: Natalie, you are so smart!

Natalie: I do know a lot of things. I know that you have dark blue eyes. I know that you smell nice all the time. I know that you love to sing and dance and that you used to wear a bra but now you don't.

If You're Not Cheating, You're Not Trying

Abby: Mommy, can you get me a pencil?

Me: Sure! What are you working on?

Abby: Homework.

Me: Honey, you did your homework last night!

Abby: Now I'm going to do Natalie's for her.

The Upside of Sleepless Nights

2:08 a.m.

Natalie: You awake, Mom?

Me: Yes.

Natalie: I just wanted to say thank you.

Me: Thank you for what?

Natalie: For everything.

Down in the Dumps

Natalie: What does it mean to get dumped?

Me: Huh?

Natalie: Like when you are on a date and you get dumped.

Me: Where did you hear that?

Natalie: Lots of places, but mostly from Lizzy.

Patterns a Plenty

Abby: We have a nice pattern going, Mom.

Me: What's that, Abby?

Abby: One day we miss the bus, the next day we don't.

Jesus, What Will They Say Next?

Abby: I can't believe we are five and a half today.

Me: I know. It's crazy how old you guys are getting. So fast.

Abby: And tomorrow is Jesus Christ's birthday.

Natalie: That's right. And it's Mommy's favorite word, too.

5 a.m.

Natalie: So, your sister is in heaven?

Me: Yeah. Yeah, Honey, she is.

Natalie: She wasn't that old though?

Me: No, Love. She wasn't. She got sick.

Natalie: Suzy didn't get sick?

Me: No.

Natalie: Johnny didn't get sick?

Me: No …

Natalie: You aren't going to get sick are you?

Me: No, Love, I try really hard not to.

Natalie: I couldn't live without my sister.

Too Much Punky Brewster?

Me: What do you girls want to do after Daddy takes you sledding today?

Abby: I was thinking maybe after we could find my birth parents.

Say as I Say

After four time-outs in two days:

Me: Abby, you are a sweet girl. Good girls do NOT say bad words like that. This is why you keep getting timed out.

Abby: I know, Mom. I'm sorry. I have an idea.

Me: What's that, Abby?

Abby: How about if you stop saying them, then I will stop saying them. Does that sound like a good idea?

Me: (sooooooo busted) Yes, Abby. That sounds like a good idea.

Abby: Pinky promise?

Me: Pinky promise.

Perspective

Abby: Big sisters can be tough.

Who Made the Cut?

Me: Natalie. Come here. Look at me.

Natalie: What?

Me: Did you cut your hair?

Natalie: No!

Me: It sure looks like you cut your hair! Did you do that at school today?

Natalie: Well, I'm not sure, and I don't have the greatest memory.

24-7 Help

4-something a.m.

Natalie: Are you awake, Momma?

Me: Aren't I always?

Natalie: Don't forget our baby pictures for school tomorrow. You forgot them today.

Me: I didn't think you were going to have school. You are right. Sorry about that.

(pause)

Natalie: Hey, Momma. If you are ever lonely, you can call me, OK?

Me: OK, Love. I will. Thank you.

Sister Secrets

On the way home from the bus stop one day, I hear whispering in the backseat:

Me: What is going on back there?

Natalie: Abby, we have to tell her.

Abby: I don't know if it's a good idea.

Me: You should probably just tell me since now I know you have something to share.

Natalie: Something terrible happened on the bus today.

Me: Spill it …

Confusing Terms

Natalie: I think I have saliva.

Me: Like in your mouth?

Natalie: Ew. No. Here on my arm.

Me: Honey, I think you might mean eczema.

Telling It Like It Is

Natalie: What are we doing this afternoon?

Me: It really depends on if I have to work or not. Why? What's up?

Natalie: Well, I was thinking maybe we could work on your style. I think we can make you a little more fashionable.

It's Not the Delivery, It's the Message

Me: Abby! What is going on these past few weeks? I feel like I keep having to say "focus, focus, focus, focus" all the time. I don't get what the problem is?

Abby: Well, I probably should have told you this awhile ago, but I don't know what the word "focus" means.

We Go Back

Natalie: Did you make this movie?

Me: No, Love. The Facebook people did.

Natalie: I love it. It really makes me remember old times.

Wearing Dresses or Uniforms?

Me: Are you girls getting excited for the daddy/daughter dance?

Abby: Yes! I can't wait!

Natalie: Are me and Abby wearing matching dresses?

Me: No, did you want to?

Natalie: I was just thinking we should because what if we get separated?

The Forgotten Reindeer/Matchmaker

Natalie: Mom, why do all the hearts on this card have arrows through them?

Me: That is because Cupid shot them with his bow and arrow.

Natalie: Who is Cupid? Is he an angel?

Me: Ummm, yeah, I think you would say that.

Abby: No offense, Natalie, but everybody knows Cupid is a reindeer.

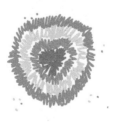

The Magic Word

Natalie: I have a nickel and a penny.

Abby: Can I have the penny?

Natalie: What's the magic word?

Abby: Please?

Natalie: Nope.

Abby: Thank you?

Natalie: Nope.

Abby: Umm … Daddy's bum stinks?

Natalie: Yep! Here you go!

Dreaming of the Big Time

Abby: Mom, when we get older can I be a ninja?

Me: Heck yeah, you can!

Sums It All Up

Abby: I know why you two laugh at each other all the time …

Me: Oh yeah, why is that?

Abby: Because you guys are in LOOOVVE!!

Me: I agree.

About the Author

Kerrie Carnes Salwa is the previous owner and operator of The Spillway, a neighborhood tavern, in the small but unique town of Clinton, located in central Massachusetts. Kerrie was born in Monroe, North Carolina, and raised in the Mentor Headlands, Ohio, outside of Cleveland. She moved to Massachusetts when she was 13. After college, Kerrie worked at the State House in Boston and the City Hall in Leominster. She currently resides in Clinton with her husband, Seth, and her twin daughters and works at a local university.

In 2010, Kerrie started a Massachusetts chapter of an organization called Breast Intentions. The group raises money year round to help local breast cancer patients pay their bills while undergoing treatment or while in recovery. Breast Intentions of MA is very dear to Kerrie's heart, so a portion of the proceeds from this book will go to Breast Intentions of MA's ongoing efforts.

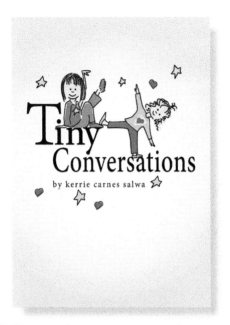

Tiny Conversations
Kerrie Carnes Salwa

www.ourtinyconversations.com

Publisher: SDP Publishing

Also available in ebook format

TO PURCHASE:
Amazon.com
BarnesAndNoble.com
SDPPublishing.com

www.SDPPublishing.com

Contact us at: info@SDPPublishing.com